The Prisoner Dilemma

Policy Options to Address Circumstances
of ISIS Prisoners in Northeastern Syria

KAREN M. SUDKAMP, HOWARD J. SHATZ,
SHELLY CULBERTSON, DOUGLAS C. LIGOR

Approved for public release; distribution unlimited

 NATIONAL SECURITY RESEARCH DIVISION

For more information on this publication, visit **www.rand.org/t/RRA2287-1**.

About RAND

The RAND Corporation is a research organization that develops solutions to public policy challenges to help make communities throughout the world safer and more secure, healthier and more prosperous. RAND is nonprofit, nonpartisan, and committed to the public interest. To learn more about RAND, visit www.rand.org.

Research Integrity

Our mission to help improve policy and decisionmaking through research and analysis is enabled through our core values of quality and objectivity and our unwavering commitment to the highest level of integrity and ethical behavior. To help ensure our research and analysis are rigorous, objective, and nonpartisan, we subject our research publications to a robust and exacting quality-assurance process; avoid both the appearance and reality of financial and other conflicts of interest through staff training, project screening, and a policy of mandatory disclosure; and pursue transparency in our research engagements through our commitment to the open publication of our research findings and recommendations, disclosure of the source of funding of published research, and policies to ensure intellectual independence. For more information, visit www.rand.org/about/principles.

RAND's publications do not necessarily reflect the opinions of its research clients and sponsors.

Published by the RAND Corporation, Santa Monica, Calif.
© 2023 RAND Corporation
RAND® is a registered trademark.

Library of Congress Cataloging-in-Publication Data is available for this publication.
ISBN: 978-1-9774-1139-6

Cover: ZUMA Press, Inc./Alamy Stock Photo.

About This Report

On July 26, 2022, the RAND Corporation hosted a roundtable discussion regarding the security and social services challenges facing the prisons that hold presumed former Islamic State of Iraq and Syria (ISIS) fighters in northeastern Syria. Three facilitated panel discussions focused on the status of legal and justice processes, resources and assistance provided to improve and maintain the security and living conditions within the prisons, and the unique challenges facing imprisoned youth. Drawing on these discussions, this report provides an overview of the situation since the territorial defeat of ISIS, identifies barriers faced by the Syrian Democratic Forces and the Defeat-ISIS Coalition, and proposes potential courses of action to reduce the security threat the prisons and prisoners present to the international community and improve the provision of social services within the prisons

The research reported here was completed in February 2023 and underwent security review with the sponsor and the Defense Office of Prepublication and Security Review before public release.

RAND National Security Research Division

This research was conducted within the International Security and Defense Policy Center of the RAND National Security Research Division (NSRD), which operates the National Defense Research Institute (NDRI), a federally funded research and development center sponsored by the Office of the Secretary of Defense, the Joint Staff, the Unified Combatant Commands, the Navy, the Marine Corps, the defense agencies, and the defense intelligence enterprise.

For more information on the RAND International Security and Defense Policy Program, see www.rand.org/nsrd/isdp or contact the director (contact information is provided on the webpage).

Funding

Funding for this research was made possible by the independent research and development provisions of RAND's contracts for the operation of its

U.S. Department of Defense federally funded research and development centers.

Acknowledgments

We especially thank our project team: Julia Doyle, Alexandra Evans, Erik E. Mueller, Jordan Reimer, Elisa Yoshiara, and Evania Baginski. Without their research and support, we would not have been able to pull off a thorough and successful summit. We appreciate Kristin Leuschner's review and editing of this report. We also thank Charles Ries of RAND and Joana Cook of Leiden University for their thorough review of this document. Abdulla Ibrahim, now of the Geneva Graduate Institute, provided invaluable assistance during the preparatory phase of the workshop. We especially thank the experts who participated in the roundtable discussion. They were promised anonymity to encourage a candid exchange of views, and we are indebted to them for sharing their knowledge. All errors remain the responsibility of the authors.

Summary

Issue

In March 2019, the Syrian Democratic Forces (SDF) with the assistance of the United States defeated the territorial caliphate of the Islamic State of Iraq and Syria (ISIS). Since then, SDF has retained approximately 10,000 presumed ISIS-affiliated men and hundreds of youths in 14 prisons across northeastern Syria. Of this total, approximately 5,000 are Syrian nationals, 3,000 are Iraqi nationals, and the remaining 2,000 are nationals from at least 58 different countries.

The prisons are insecure, and ISIS has a longstanding goal—achieved, at least in part, in January 2022 in al-Hasakeh, Syria, for example—of conducting prison attacks to release its members. The prisons place a drain on SDF, the first line of defense against the ISIS remnants in northeast Syria. The prisoners are left in a legal limbo, with no internationally agreed-on justice procedures to determine their fate and few countries willing to repatriate their nationals. These prisons present a danger to the region and the world given their potential for fueling an ISIS resurgence.

Approach

The RAND Corporation gathered 18 external subject-matter experts and RAND associates at a policy summit in July 2022. The purpose of this summit was to gain insights into the current situation in the prisons, to understand the most critical problems and risks posed by this situation, to identify barriers to addressing these problems and risks, and to propose solutions. In addition, RAND conducted a literature review about these issues.

Key Findings

The discussion at the policy summit revealed that the situation of the ISIS prisoners carries four problems and risks.

- Participants emphasized that the risk of a prison breakout is the most critical security threat from the current situation.
- Guarding the prisons is a challenge. While SDF and other security organizations of the Autonomous Administration of North and East Syria (the de facto governing authority) receive some training, more is needed.
- Conditions within the prisons and the treatment of prisoners present an additional risk as the poor conditions do not meet international norms for treatment of prisoners, exacerbate humanitarian and public health concerns, and have led to riots. In addition, these conditions could provide fodder for ISIS messaging about mistreatment by SDF and the Defeat-ISIS (D-ISIS) Coalition, the multinational alliance that fought ISIS and remains together to prevent ISIS's return.
- Finally, the prisoners include youth in conditions that do not accord with humanitarian norms and standards of care for children and could lead to greater risk of their radicalization.

There are several barriers to addressing these problems and mitigating these risks.

- SDF is guarding the prisons with only limited resources. It is likely that many prisoners will remain for a long period, yet the resources needed to support the long-term presence of the prisoners (sufficient security and standard-meeting conditions for the prisoners) have not been allocated by the international community or available for either the immediate term or the longer term.
- Home countries hesitate to repatriate prisoners, presumed ISIS fighters, although some countries are repatriating ISIS-linked women and children residing in displacement camps in northeastern Syria.
- There is ongoing instability in northeastern Syria (including an attack on the area by Turkey) and no settlement to the country's civil war. Consequently, SDF often must direct its resources to problems other than the prisons.
- Finally, there is no agreed-on justice process for the prisoners or juvenile justice process for the youth. Evidence collection to support justice procedures is also lacking.

Recommendations

The policy summit discussion identified a set of steps for the short term (within one year) and for the medium term (within two to five years) that could solve some of the problems presented by the prisons and mitigate some of the risks.

The following short-term courses of action emerged from the discussion:

- Recognize that many of the prisoners are likely to be incarcerated in northeastern Syria over the long term. Conducting a census of prisoners would provide SDF and the D-ISIS Coalition a better understanding of the prison population and its needs. Further, a security assessment would allow SDF and the D-ISIS Coalition to better understand threats and set priorities to mitigate them.
- Continue efforts to encourage repatriation of foreign prisoners. Separate inducements might be needed for European nationals and for other non-Iraqi foreign nationals. Iraq has indicated willingness to take back its nationals and has done so on a modest scale, but additional identification of capacities, barriers, and investments is required.
- Develop justice processes. There are a variety of possible options, but agreement on which to choose would help create incentive to bring presumed ISIS fighters to justice.
- Move youth from prisons to facilities designed to support their unique needs with humane conditions, healthcare, and education. As of late 2022, a new facility had been developed in Qamishli that could accommodate prisoners who are minors, but SDF claimed a lack of resources to implement new solutions, and the exact status of the facility was unclear.

The following medium-term courses of action emerged from discussion:

- Construct purpose-built prisons that meet international standards while continuing to professionalize security forces. This is related to the recognition that many of the prisoners will remain in place for years to come; failure to build prisons will not change that reality but will raise security risks.

- Implement the repatriation and justice processes that reflect international standards as prescribed within the shorter-term courses of action.
- Determine exit pathways for youth from the youth-oriented facility to which they have been moved. This will involve providing education or training, as well as documentation attesting to their education and identity. The main obstacle is likely to be the possibility that no country is willing to take them, meaning that many must build lives in Syria.

Our policy summit discussions suggested that there are potential solutions to the prisoner dilemma and that a plan for working towards such solutions can be created, with short-term actions and medium-term policy directions. A grand coalition of local and international forces defeated ISIS, and follow-up by that coalition is needed to ensure the terrorist group does not return.

Contents

Figure

CHAPTER 1

Introduction: The Problem

In March 2019, the Syrian Democratic Forces (SDF) reclaimed the town of Baghouz, Syria, from the Islamic State of Iraq and Syria (ISIS), thereby territorially defeating the organization's so-called caliphate.[1] Baghouz was the final holding of ISIS, and approximately 50,000 to 60,000 ISIS fighters and their families emerged over the ten-week battle, exceeding U.S. and SDF estimates of the remaining size of the group within the town.[2] U.S. forces within the Global Coalition to Defeat-ISIS (D-ISIS) supported SDF as it separated the ISIS-related people into two groups and sent them to separate destinations within northeastern Syria.[3] Women and children went to existing camps that shelter refugees and internally displaced persons (IDPs) (such as al-Hol), and men went to makeshift prisons.[4]

Since then, SDF has retained approximately 10,000 presumed ISIS-affiliated men in 14 prisons across northeastern Syria.[5] Of this total,

---

[1] The organization has also been known as ISIL (for Islamic State of Iraq and the Levant) and Da'esh (the acronym of its Arabic name).

[2] Michael R. Gordon, *Degrade and Destroy: The Inside Story of the War Against the Islamic State, from Barack Obama to Donald Trump*, Farrar, Straus, and Giroux, 2022.

[3] When established by the Obama administration, the name used was the Global Coalition to Counter ISIS; however, the Trump administration changed "counter" to "defeat" and the Biden administration has retained this terminology.

[4] Gordon, 2022; Rodi Said, "Islamic State 'Caliphate' Defeated, Yet Threat Persists," Reuters, March 23, 2019.

[5] Lead Inspector General, *Operation Inherent Resolve: Lead Inspector General Report to the United States Congress, January 1, 2022–March 31, 2022*, U.S. Department of Defense, May 3, 2022b.

approximately 5,000 are Syrian nationals and 3,000 are Iraqi nationals.[6] The remaining 2,000 are nationals from at least 58 different countries, with approximately 800 of these from Europe and most of the rest from the Middle East and North Africa.[7] It remains unclear how many prisoners at these locations are not ISIS-affiliated and whether they are separated from the ISIS-affiliated population. As of mid-2021, the al-Hasakeh Central Prison held both ISIS prisoners and "common criminals," for example.[8] Critically, the presumed ISIS-affiliated fighters currently held have not been charged or convicted of crimes and yet face indefinite imprisonment. Of particular concern are at least 700 boys aged 10 to 17 (in 2019) who were imprisoned following the fall of Baghouz; UNICEF reported that by January 2022, 850 children were held in detention without having been charged with crimes.[9] Their presence in the prisons was highlighted during ISIS's January 2022 attack on the Ghuwayran Detention Facility in al-Hasakeh, when the boys were caught in the fighting and used as human shields.[10]

---

[6] Charlie Savage, "ISIS Fighters' Children Are Growing Up in a Desert Camp. What Will They Become?" *New York Times*, July 19, 2022; Lead Inspector General, *Operation Inherent Resolve: Lead Inspector General Report to the United States Congress, July 1, 2020–September 30, 2020*, U.S. Department of Defense, November 3, 2020b; Lead Inspector General, 2022b; Lead Inspector General, *Operation Inherent Resolve: Lead Inspector General Report to the United States Congress, April 1, 2022–June 30, 2022*, U.S. Department of Defense, July 29, 2022c.

[7] Savage, 2022; "Syria Kurds Free More Than 600 ISIL Fighters as Part of Amnesty," *Al Jazeera*, October 15, 2020; Andrew Hanna, "Islamists Imprisoned Across the Middle East," Wilson Center, June 24, 2021.

[8] Lead Inspector General, *Operation Inherent Resolve: Lead Inspector General Report to the United States Congress, July 1, 2021–September 30, 2021*, U.S. Department of Defense, November 3, 2021, p. 76.

[9] Lead Inspector General, 2022b; Henrietta Fore, "Children Caught Up in al-Hasakeh Prison Violence Must Be Evacuated to Safety," press release, United Nations Children's Fund, January 25, 2022.

[10] This prison is also referred to as the al-Sina'a Detention Facility, which is located in the Ghuwayran neighborhood of al-Hasakeh. We will refer to this prison as Ghuwayran in this report. Louisa Loveluck and Sarah Cahlan, "Prison Break: ISIS Fighters Launched a Brazen Attack to Free Their Comrades," *Washington Post*, February 3, 2022; "Calls to Evacuate 700 Boys from Syria's Guweiran Prison Due to Intense Fighting," press release, Save the Children, January 24, 2022; Jane Arraf and Sangar Khaleel,

The presumed ISIS-affiliated fighters represent a potential risk to regional and international security if they leave the prisons and rejoin ISIS. In addition, the conditions in which they are held do not meet global minimum standards for treatment of prisoners, reflecting poorly on the D-ISIS Coalition[11] and its SDF partners.[12] According to the U.S. Department of Defense (DoD):

> The detainee population represents the largest concentration of ISIS fighters globally, and the protection and management of these detainees remains critical to preventing an ISIS resurgence. If not effectively contained, these ISIS fighters could re-emerge as a committed and experienced fighting force applied against Coalition and partner forces.[13]

Holding ISIS fighters and other known and suspected affiliates in substandard prisons can lead to further indoctrination and radicalization among prisoners, runs counter to values prescribed by the D-ISIS Coalition, and places a drain on the personnel resources of SDF, the first line of defense against an ISIS resurgence in northeast Syria.

At the same time, for those who remain imprisoned, the poor state of the prison infrastructure, along with the substandard conditions for the prisoners (especially the boys), increases security and health risks. These prisons are overcrowded and often ad hoc structures, adapted quickly to hold the unexpected influx of men and boys. For example, at Ghuwayran, between 100 to 150 prisoners have been reported to share a cell, leading to approxi-

---

"Teenage Inmates Found Among the 500 Dead in Syria Prison Attack," *New York Times*, January 31, 2022.

[11] The 85 coalition members are listed in U.S. Department of State, "Members—The Global Coalition to Defeat ISIS," webpage, undated. These include countries and security institutions in Africa, the Americas, Asia-Pacific, Europe, and the Middle East.

[12] See generally, United Nations Office of the High Commissioner for Human Rights, "International Standards on Detention," webpage, undated.

[13] Office of the Secretary of Defense, *Department of Defense Budget Fiscal Year (FY) 2023: Justification for FY 2023 Overseas Operations Counter-Islamic State of Iraq and Syria (ISIS) Train and Equip Fund (CTEF)*, U.S. Department of Defense, April 2022.

mately 0.6 square meters of living space per person.[14] Prison conditions that do not adhere to accepted international standards can serve as a propaganda tool against counter-ISIS forces and the West more generally. Furthermore, the detention of children in these conditions does not meet international standards for detainment of minors and stands in violation of the rights of the child.[15] While many of the issues associated with indefinite imprisonment overlap between adult and juvenile detention, the impacts and potential solutions vary between the two age groups.

The treatment of prisoners in these prisons and associated security risks are well-understood. The Autonomous Administration of North and East Syria (AANES)—the local governing and security authority—along with U.S., European, and Middle Eastern government and security officials and international humanitarian nongovernmental organizations (NGOs), acknowledge both the potential threat to global security posed by the ISIS-affiliated prisoners and the living conditions within the prisons. Multiple solutions have been proposed, ranging from new purpose-built prisons to training for SDF to bringing presumed-ISIS fighters to justice and repatriating third-country nationals. The United States continues to urge partners and allies to address the situation, with Secretary of State Antony Blinken stating in June 2021, "This situation is simply untenable. It just can't persist indefinitely."[16]

Despite such intentions, as well as U.S funding, training, and expertise, the situation with the prisons, while improving, remains a risk and does not reliably support the stabilization of the post-ISIS environment. This impasse reflects not a lack of understanding, but of political will and attention. Further, the problem is not likely to resolve itself anytime soon. The most likely

---

[14] Lead Inspector General, 2022b.

[15] Fionnuala Ní Aoláin, "Position of the United Nations Special Rapporteur on the Promotion and Protection of Human Rights and Fundamental Freedoms While Countering Terrorism on the Human Rights of Adolescents/Juveniles Being Detained in North-East Syria," United Nations Human Rights Special Procedures, May 2021; United Nations, *United Nations Standard Minimum Rules for the Administration of Juvenile Justice (The Beijing Rules)*, Adopted by General Assembly Resolution 40/33 of November 29, 1985.

[16] Antony J. Blinken, "Secretary Antony J. Blinken Opening Remarks at D-ISIS Meeting Opening Session," ministerial meeting of the Global Coalition to Defeat ISIS, Rome, Italy, June 28, 2021.

Relationship to the Syrian Civil War

The counter-ISIS campaign began in 2013, situated within the broader context of the Syrian Civil War, which began in March 2011. The Syrian regime, supported by Russia, Iran, Lebanese Hizballah and other Iranian-backed militia groups, has focused predominantly on putting down the uprising in the western portion of Syria. SDF, supported by the D-ISIS Coalition, has been the primary force fighting ISIS in the eastern part of the country. However, since mid-2019, Syrian, Russian, and Iranian-backed militias have gradually increased activity in southeastern Syria, particularly in Deir-ez-Zor Governorate and the Middle Euphrates River Valley, increasing adversarial actions between the regime and its supporters and SDF and the D-ISIS Coalition. While the most active fighting had ceased by early 2023 with the regime in control of most of the country, an uneasy stalemate remains as there has been no political solution to end hostilities.

scenario facing AANES, SDF, the United States, and the D-ISIS Coalition, is that the prisoners will be there for some time. A best-case estimate is five to 10 years but, considering the territorial defeat of ISIS occurred in 2019 and limited attention is currently given to implementing solutions, some of these men could be imprisoned indefinitely—effectively for the rest of their lives, unless the weak prison security leads to a successful prison break.

Focus of This Report

On July 26, 2022, the RAND Corporation gathered 18 RAND associates and external subject-matter experts at a policy summit to discuss the security risks and substandard prison conditions associated with the continued, presumed to be indefinite, imprisonment of ISIS-affiliated fighters in northeastern Syria.[17] The purpose of this summit was to gain insights into the current situation in the prisons, to understand the most critical problems and risks posed by this situation, to identify barriers to addressing these problems and risks, and to propose immediate- and medium-term courses of action.

---

[17] All data used for this report were current as of September 2022 and were not updated prior to the release of the report.

Methods

At the policy summit, the RAND team first presented an overview of available literature from publicly available U.S. government documents and policymaker comments, reports from research organizations and international nongovernmental organizations (NGOs), and journalist articles on this issue as background and a foundation for the discussion. Discussions were thematically focused on several general subject areas: justice processes, youth detention, and provision of security assistance and social services. Sessions focused on the following questions:

- How can prison populations be reduced?
- How can repatriations and returns be facilitated in Iraq, Syria, and internationally?
- How can the unique needs of youth be addressed?
- How can resources be provided to improve security and social services at the prisons?

A roundtable discussion then took place under the Chatham House Rule with representatives from research institutions, universities, and NGOs. Many of these participants had in-country experience with the situation, and some were former government officials who worked on the issue. For each discussion, a member of the RAND team presented a scene-setting briefing based on the literature review, and then two or three participants, depending on the topic, presented introductory remarks. Following those introductory remarks, a member of the RAND team moderated a discussion. Three members of the RAND project team took notes.

Our goal with the policy summit was to arrive at courses of action for the international community to solve the problems presented by the ISIS prisons and to mitigate the risks. To do so, moderators guided each discussion to focus on solutions. Throughout the discussion, there was general agreement among the participants regarding both problems and solutions. In instances where differences in opinion or previously unconsidered solutions were raised, moderators questioned participants to identify the central aspects of the differing perspectives or solutions; these are noted in the following chapters. The suggested solutions formed the core of the courses of action we report in Chapter 4. The RAND team took those solutions and

Prisons Versus Detention Centers

In this report we use the terms "prisoners" and "prisons" as opposed to "detainees" and "detention centers," unless we are quoting official documents using the latter terms. Throughout the literature and during our roundtable discussion, both terms are used frequently.

conducted further, limited research to understand whether the international community was taking any action regarding those solutions—and if so, what actions—and whether those solutions presented any challenges beyond those raised in the policy summit.

Organization of This Report

This report presents the findings of the literature overview prepared for the policy summit, the summit discussion and conclusions, and additional information to round out the summit discussions and conclusions. The report is organized into five chapters, including this chapter. Chapter 2 describes the circumstances at the prisons and lay out the problems and risks associated with the status quo. Chapter 3 describes barriers to taking action to address these problems and risks. Chapter 4 describes short-term courses of action and medium-term policy directions, and Chapter 5 offers concluding thoughts.

CHAPTER 2

The Current Status of the ISIS Prisons

Prison Locations and Environment

As of summer 2022, Syria was a divided country with four zones of control. The government of Syria—the Assad regime—controlled the largest portion, specifically most of the west and areas south of the Euphrates. Turkish-backed forces controlled areas along the Turkish border stemming from several Turkish military operations from 2016 to 2019. The province of Idlib in the northwest hosted millions of IDPs and was controlled by several armed groups, the most dominant of which was Hay'at Tahrir al-Sham, which at one time was a formal al-Qa'ida affiliate. And finally, most of three provinces in the northeast north of the Euphrates were governed by the Kurdish-dominated AANES with the Kurdish-dominated SDF as the military force. It is AANES (not internationally recognized as a sovereign government) and SDF (not recognized as a national military force of a sovereign government or state) that are responsible for the ISIS prisons.[1]

As noted previously, the unexpectedly high numbers of ISIS fighters and their families surprised SDF and partnered U.S. forces after the fall of Baghouz, and the necessary prisons were established or renovated quickly; they remain "ad hoc" and "overcrowded."[2] For example, a prison in Ain Issa

[1] Philip Loft, *Syria and Its Civil War: A Future Under Assad?* Commons Library Research Briefing Number 9378, House of Commons Library, United Kingdom, November 26, 2021.

[2] Lead Inspector General, 2020b, p. 52.

in Raqqa Governorate is a converted and hardened school.[3] The detention facility at al-Hasakeh Central Prison is the only "improved and hardened purpose-built" detention facility that is "built well enough to serve as a long-term detention facility."[4] This facility, along with another in the city of ash-Shaddadi, holds approximately two-thirds of the ISIS-affiliated prisoners.[5] The other major SDF jails are located in Malikiya, Qamishli, and Tabqa.[6] Figure 2.1 shows the locations of the prisons and displaced persons camps in northeastern Syria.

SDF's Provincial Internal Security Forces (PrISF) is the primary provider of security at SDF prisons. They receive some support from other SDF elements, including Internal Security Forces (InSF) and SDF military intelligence.[7] The D-ISIS Coalition, working predominantly through the United States, provides funding and training to SDF to secure and harden the prisons and train SDF to run the facilities. DoD's budget request for fiscal year (FY) 2023 includes allocations for basic life support services, stipends, prison construction support, guard and security force training, and sustainment to address security gaps and support SDF units guarding the prisons.[8] Over the course of 2022, DoD reportedly planned to spend a total of $155 million to train and equip SDF, which includes improving prison infrastructure; however, exact figures specifically for the prisons are publicly unknown.[9]

---

[3] Charlie Savage, "As ISIS Fighters Fill Prisons in Syria, Their Home Nations Look Away," *New York Times*, July 18, 2018.

[4] Lead Inspector General, 2020b, p. 52.

[5] Lead Inspector General, 2021.

[6] Hanna, 2021.

[7] Lead Inspector General, *Operation Inherent Resolve: Lead Inspector General Report to the United States Congress, October 1, 2021–December 31, 2021*, U.S. Department of Defense, February 8, 2022a.

[8] Office of the Secretary of Defense, 2022.

[9] Savage, 2022.

FIGURE 2.1

Locations of SDF-Run Prisons in Northeastern Syria

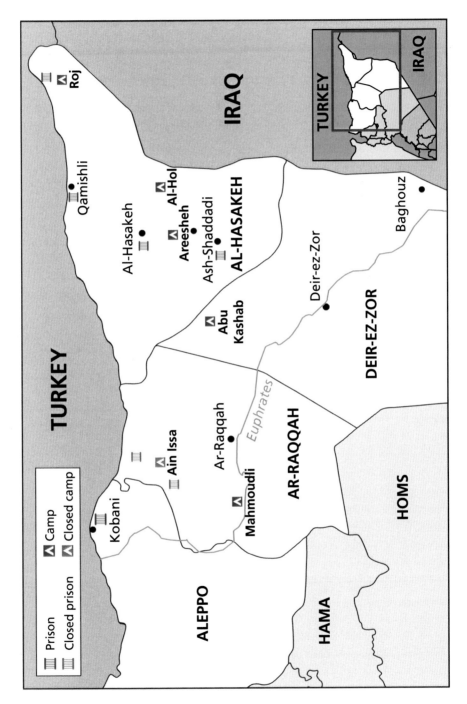

Problems and Risks

Participants in the policy summit emphasized four critical problems associated with the current situation in the ISIS prisons.

Prison Breakouts Remain a Constant Risk

Participants emphasized that the risk of a prison breakout is the most critical risk from the current situation. A successful breakout would provide a reinforcement of trained fighters to ISIS and would serve as a major propaganda victory for the group. Breakouts can also lead to tension between SDF, the United States, and the D-ISIS Coalition. The fact that most of the prisons holding ISIS and presumed ISIS members were not purpose-built adds to the risk of breakouts. Such facilities are harder to secure and harden (thus more prone to riots and breakouts), and they are in locations that are closer to civilians, raising the potential for civilian harm.

Prison breakouts are a long-standing ISIS technique. Freeing prisoners and taking care of the families of imprisoned ISIS members is part of formal doctrine promulgated by the group and its predecessors.[10] ISIS leadership maintains a minister (an *emir*) of prisoners and detainees.[11] These principles have been articulated and acted upon many times. As early as 2005, ISIS predecessor al-Qa'ida in Iraq attempted to free prisoners from Abu Ghraib prison.[12] In 2012, then-ISIS leader Abu Bakr al-Baghdadi launched the Breaking the Walls campaign, which resulted in seven attacks on a total of eight Iraqi prisons from July 2012 to July 2013, freeing an estimated 600

---

[10] Brian Fishman, *Fourth Generation Governance—Sheikh Tamimi Defends the Islamic State of Iraq*, Combating Terrorism Center, West Point, March 23, 2007; Bennett Clifford and Caleb Weiss, "'Breaking the Walls' Goes Global: The Evolving Threat of Jihadi Prison Assaults and Riots," *Combating Terrorism Center Sentinel*, Vol. 13, No. 2, February 2020.

[11] Hisham al-Hashimi, Telegraph Interactive Team, and Ruth Sherlock, "Revealed: The Islamic State 'Cabinet,' from Finance Minister to Suicide Bomb Deployer," *The Telegraph*, July 9, 2014; Charles Lister, "Who's Who of the Islamic State Senior Leadership," in *Profiling the Islamic State*, Brookings Institution, December 1, 2014.

[12] Jessica Lewis, "Al Qaeda in Iraq's 'Breaking the Walls' Campaign Achieves Its Objectives at Abu Ghraib," 2013 Iraq Update #30, Institute for the Study of War, July 28, 2013.

fighters.[13] In 2019, he then launched the Breaking the Fortress strategy of prison breakouts.[14] More recently, in August 2020, the Afghanistan branch of ISIS known as Islamic State Khorasan Province, attacked a prison in Jalalabad, freeing an estimated 270 ISIS fighters; it is not clear how many were recaptured subsequently.[15] In October 2020, the ISIS affiliate in the Democratic Republic of Congo, known as the Allied Democratic Forces, attacked the Kangbayi prison in the town of Beni, freeing 1,300 prisoners, an undetermined number of whom were ISIS members.[16]

A major attack on and breakout from—and 10-day battle at—Ghuwayran prison in January 2022 reminded the world that the threat of ISIS fighters breaking out and working to reignite an ISIS reign of terror remains a possibility.[17] Two other riots occurred within the same prison in September 2020,[18] while, in November 2021, SDF foiled another ISIS breakout attempt.[19] Following the January 2022 attack, the United States spent over $3 million to refurbish buildings within the Ghuwayran complex, purchase a closed-circuit television security system, and support other efforts to maintain the "secure and humane" detention of ISIS fighters to address the structural damage to the facility.[20]

---

[13] Lewis, 2013.

[14] Jared Malsin and Benoit Faucon, "Islamic State Plotted Comeback Long Before Syria Prison Attack," *Wall Street Journal*, January 28, 2022.

[15] Noorullah Shirzada and Elise Blanchard, "Islamic State Jihadists on the Run After Afghan Prison Raid," AFP, August 4, 2020.

[16] Caleb Weiss, "Islamic State Claims Prison Break in the DRC," *Long War Journal*, Foundation for Defense of Democracies, October 20, 2020.

[17] Loveluck and Cahlan, 2022; Louisa Loveluck, "The World Forgot This Syrian Prison. The Islamic State Did Not." *Washington Post*, February 5, 2022.

[18] Lead Inspector General, 2020b.

[19] Lead Inspector General, 2022a.

[20] Lead Inspector General, 2022b, p. 69.

SDF Staffing Constraints Add to Security Challenges

Guarding the ISIS prisons is a challenge. While PrISF, InSF, and SDF military intelligence guards receive some training, more is needed.[21] To date, efforts have focused on training the PrISF that guard two prisons in al-Hasakeh and ash-Shaddadi. Training has included the "use of pepper spray, riot shields, and batons" to better "quell riots and ensure the secure detention of ISIS detainees."[22] In its FY 2023 budget request, DoD asked for funding to expand the number of guards at prisons and train them with the goal of improving both security and humane treatment of the prisoners.[23]

SDF faces other security challenges that can result in understaffing of the prisons. These include ISIS activity throughout the northeast, interference by Syrian and Russian troops, and attacks and interference by Iranian-linked militias.[24] The direst security challenge may be the threat of a renewed attack by Turkey, an action that could lead SDF to pull personnel from the prisons and redirect them to the battlefield. During Turkey's October 2019 incursion into northeast Syria, called Operation Peace Spring, either due to Turkish shelling, a drawdown of guards to escape the shelling, or other reasons, an estimated "dozens" of ISIS prisoners escaped.[25] In addition, such an attack could draw SDF forces from countering ISIS, giving more room to that group to attack prisons. During Operation Peace Spring, SDF stopped counter-ISIS activity.[26] Furthermore, SDF temporarily lowered

---

[21] Lead Inspector General, 2022a.

[22] Lead Inspector General, 2022a, p. 76.

[23] Office of the Secretary of Defense, 2022.

[24] For challenges from Russia, see Khaled al-Khateb, "Is Russia Extorting SDF in Northeast Syria?" *Al-Monitor*, February 26, 2021. For challenges from Iranian-linked militias, see Combined Joint Task Force—Operation Inherent Resolve, "Coalition: Iran-Backed Militia Attacks a Dangerous Distraction from Mission," January 5, 2022; Mohammed Hassan and Samer al-Ahmed, "Iran's Growing Presence in Syria's al-Hasakeh Poses a Direct Threat to U.S. Forces," Middle East Institute, March 24, 2022.

[25] James Jeffrey, "Assessing the Impact of Turkey's Offensive in Northeast Syria," Hearing before the Committee on Foreign Relations, United States Senate, Senate Hearing 116-109, October 22, 2019, p. 25.

[26] Lead Inspector General, *Operation Inherent Resolve: Lead Inspector General Report to the United States Congress, October 1, 2019–December 31, 2019*, U.S. Department of

the number of personnel stationed at IDP camps, leading to the departure of ISIS-affiliated families, although it is not clear it did so at the prisons housing ISIS fighters.[27]

Treatment of Prisoners Does Not Meet D-ISIS Coalition Standards and Can Amplify Anti-Western Narratives

Conditions within the prisons and the treatment of prisoners present an additional risk as the poor conditions exacerbate humanitarian and public health concerns and lead to security complications. Prisoners rioted three times in 2020—March, May, and June—over fears of potential infection with coronavirus disease 2019 (COVID-19).[28] Boys and teenagers in the prisons may be especially vulnerable to physical and mental health diseases; it has been reported they are undernourished, exposed to diseases such as human immunodeficiency virus (HIV) and tuberculosis, have limited outdoor access, display signs of emotional distress, and lack regular contact with their families.[29]

Substandard conditions also reinforce a "narrative of grievances caused by Western governments," potentially leading to greater radicalization among the prisoners or furthering efforts to riot, protest, or break out.[30] ISIS predecessor the Islamic State of Iraq, itself the successor to al-Qa'ida in Iraq,

---

Defense, February 4, 2020a.

[27] Lead Inspector General, 2020a. Turkey is at odds with the AANES and the SDF military force because it believes SDF is part of the Kurdistan Workers Party (PKK), a Turkish Kurdish group with which Turkey has been in conflict since the 1980s. Both the United States and Turkey have deemed the PKK a terrorist group. And, in fact, the United States has agreed that SDF is, at minimum, linked to the PKK. In 2019, a senior State Department official said, " . . . we need a partner on the ground. That partner has been SDF, a major component of which has been the YPG [the Syrian Kurdish People's Protection Units], which is the Syrian offshoot of the PKK." See Cameron Abadi, "Why Is Turkey Fighting Syria's Kurds?" *Foreign Policy*, October 17, 2019; U.S. Department of State, "Senior State Department Officials on the Situation in Syria," briefing, Office of the Spokesperson, October 10, 2019.

[28] Hanna, 2021.

[29] Lead Inspector General, 2022b.

[30] Eric Oehlerich, Mick Mulroy, and Liam McHugh, *Jannah or Jahannam: Options for Dealing with ISIS Detainees*, Middle East Institute, October 13, 2020, pp. 4–5.

used sectarian grievances as a tool to strengthen the group's appeal in 2006. Such grievances provided acceptance of, if not support for, ISIS as it conquered parts of Iraq and Syria in 2013 onward.[31] Crowded conditions and extended imprisonment without a clear next step could also provide opportunities for indoctrination and planning by the most radical elements.[32]

Moreover, the prisons are not living up to international norms and commitments related to conditions and standards established by the United Nations (UN) and commonly known as the Mandela Rules.[33] These standards address such issues as prisoner treatment and respect, providing for due process, prison management, humane accommodations, guidance related discipline, and external contact.[34] Adherence to these standards is intended to benefit the global community; indeed, the promotion of these international norms and values was a key communication point in the counter-ISIS campaign from 2014 onward, which contrasted with the brutality of life in the so-called ISIS caliphate.[35]

Youth Are Imprisoned with Adults

A fourth problem concerns the continued imprisonment of the youth in conditions that do not accord with humanitarian norms and standards of care for children, as well as their risk of radicalization.[36] One major prob-

---

[31] Patrick B. Johnston, Jacob N. Shapiro, Howard J. Shatz, Benjamin Bahney, Danielle F. Jung, Patrick K. Ryan, and Jonathan Wallace, *Foundations of the Islamic State: Management, Money, and Terror in Iraq, 2005–2010*, RAND Corporation, RR-1192-DARPA, 2016.

[32] Oehlerich, Mulroy, and McHugh, 2020.

[33] United Nations General Assembly, *The United Nations Standard Minimum Rules for Treatment of Prisoners (the Nelson Mandela Rules)*, adopted by the General Assembly Resolution 70/175 of December 17, 2015. See also United Nations Office of the High Commissioner for Human Rights, 2022.

[34] Andrew Gilmour, "The Nelson Mandela Rules: Protecting the Rights of Persons Deprived of Liberty," *United Nations Chronicle*, undated.

[35] United Nations Security Council, "ISIL/Da'esh Committed Genocide of Yazidi, War Crimes Against Unarmed Cadets, Military Personnel in Iraq, Investigative Team Head Tells Security Council," press release, May 10, 2021.

[36] See United Nations, 1985.

lem is that these boys, ages 12 through 17, are at a formative stage of life in terrible conditions. Current levels of protection and educational opportunities for youth in prison are insufficient and are not in line with the rights of the child and principles of juvenile justice.[37] NGOs complain that SDF will not allow access to or medical support for youth in the prisons. Education is limited, poor, or nonexistent. Fionnuala Ní Aoláin, the UN Special Rapporteur on the promotion and protection of human rights while countering terrorism reported that the situation "beggars belief."[38] Her report documented prison conditions for these children:

> . . . abhorrent conditions including inadequate shelter, no bedding provision, unmanaged overcrowding, no access to sunlight, insufficient latrine access and virtually no shower access. Malnourishment is rife. Boys held in these facilities suffer from scabies and other skin conditions, they are vulnerable to HIV, Tuberculosis, and COVID-19 exposure. Boys in these detention facilities endure untreated war injuries, missing limbs, and severe trauma. These conditions meet the threshold for torture, inhuman and degrading treatment under international law, and no child should have to endure them. The de facto culling, separation, and warehousing of adolescent boys from their mothers is an abhorrent practice inconsistent with the dignity of the boy child.[39]

Notably, there is at least one separate youth detention center (and possibly more), but as with the prisons, the conditions there appear to be difficult and need further investment, money for which had not yet been provided as of the end of 2021.[40] Moreover, this center may not even be operational, according to our participants.

---

[37] United Nations, *Convention on the Rights of the Child*, Adopted by General Assembly Resolution 44/26 of November 20, 1989.

[38] "Syria: 700 Child Detainees Held in Prison Under Siege," UN News, January 25, 2022.

[39] Ní Aoláin, 2021, p. 3.

[40] Heather Murdock, "Foreign Children of IS Detained in Northeast Syria Face Bleak Future," *VOA*, November 4, 2021; Lead Inspector General, 2022a.

In addition, the children have not been charged with specific crimes or tried. Lack of a process to resolve their status violates principles of juvenile justice.[41]

A separate problem is that if the men (or even older boys) have access to youth, the younger boys could be subject to physical, sexual, and mental abuse or radicalization. ISIS has a track record of turning boys into fighters, especially through its so-called Cubs of the Caliphate program.[42]

There are uncertainties surrounding the scope of the problem. It is not clear how many youth ages 12 and above are in the prisons. Differing reports in 2022 place the number between 700 and 850.[43] However, other reports said that while 700 were brought to that prison in 2019, the numbers have since decreased, potentially as a result of boys aging into adulthood.[44] Adding to the complication, some boys have been shifted to the prisons from camps such as al-Hol and Roj, adding to the youth prison population.[45] In addition, while youth are reportedly held separately from men, we do not have visibility into whether the two populations have opportunities to mix, nor do we have complete information on whether youth who reach age 18 are then mixed with the men.[46]

---

[41] See United Nations, 1985.

[42] Jamie Dettmer, "Steeped in Martyrdom, Cubs of the Caliphate Groomed as Jihadist Legacy," VOA, July 6, 2017.

[43] "Syria: 700 Child Detainees Held in Prison Under Siege," 2022; Fore, 2022.

[44] Lead Inspector General, 2022b.

[45] Ní Aoláin, 2021.

[46] Youth reaching age 18 is cited as a factor in the decline of the total number of young people in detention. See Lead Inspector General, 2022b.

CHAPTER 3

Barriers to Addressing Problems and Risks Presented by ISIS Prisons

Finding acceptable solutions to the problems and risks presented by ISIS will be difficult, and the challenge of implementing solutions is made more severe because of institutional and political barriers. Participants in the policy summit identified four key barriers that are impeding progress, as described below.

Limited Resources

It is likely that there will be a large ISIS prison population held in northeast Syria indefinitely—or at least until an international adjudicative system is developed and implemented that would facilitate repatriation of prisoners to other countries. However, the resources needed to support the long-term presence of the prisoners (sufficient security and standard-meeting conditions for the prisoners) have not been allocated or available for either the short or long term. SDF depends on foreign aid to pay for prison operations, including training, uniforms, equipment, medical supplies, food, and water. While the D-ISIS Coalition has funded construction and refurbishment projects aimed at increasing the security and capacity of the prisons, these efforts have so far proved insufficient for both humane treatment and security.

SDF would need long-term commitments from the United States and multilateral partners to support the sustainability of ISIS prisons. The United States is currently constrained in this sense by the appropriation methods the United States uses to provide support to SDF; the CTEF by law must be used to aid Syrian forces in the military defeat of ISIS.[1] CTEF funds can be used to provide "training, equipment, logistics support, supplies, and services[;] stipends, facility and infrastructure repair and renovation[;] and sustainment to Iraq, including Kurdish and tribal security forces, or other local security forces fighting ISIS in Iraq and Syria."[2] For example, CTEF funds can be used for the training and sustainment of prison guards, including training related to the treatment of prisoners, but not applied to improving the prisoners' living conditions.[3] Additionally, CTEF funds might lawfully be allocated to refurbish buildings, although it likely would not be legally permissible to apply such funds to new construction, including purpose-built prisons.[4]

In addition, although a new facility has been developed in Qamishli that could accommodate prisoners who are minors, SDF claims a lack of resources to implement new solutions, and public information provides an unclear picture of the situation with this facility.

Unwillingness or Inability of Home Countries to Repatriate Prisoners

Another barrier involves the limited number of non-Syrian prisoners who have been repatriated to their home countries. While 4,000 to 5,000 prisoners are of Syrian origin, a similar number are nationals of other coun-

---

[1] The fund was established by merging Sections 1209 and 1236 of the 2015 National Defense Authorization Act (P.L.113-291). Section 1209 provides support to vetted Syrian opposition groups, such as SDF, and Section 1236 governs the support provided to Iraqi Security Forces. See U.S. Department of Defense Inspector General, *Audit of the DoD's Accountability of the Counter-Islamic State of Iraq and Syria Train and Equip Fund Equipment Designated for Syria*, Department of Defense, DODIG-2020-061, February 13, 2020.

[2] U.S. Department of Defense and U.S. Department of State, *Foreign Military Training Report, Fiscal Years 2020 and 2021: Joint Report to Congress, Volume 1*, October 18, 2021, p. II–7.

[3] Office of the Secretary of Defense, 2022.

[4] See Carla E. Humud, "Syria and U.S. Policy," Congressional Research Service, IF 11930, updated April 19, 2022.

tries.[5] Three thousand are Iraqis, while the remaining 2,000 are from other countries. Repatriation has been recognized as an important potential solution. The Office of the Under Secretary of Defense for Policy, International Security Affairs (ISA) has said that the United States continues to view repatriation of foreign prisoners as the "best long-term option to decrease overcrowding" in SDF prisons.[6] Similarly, former U.S. Central Command commander Gen Kenneth F. McKenzie, Jr., said in early 2022 that the slow repatriation and reintegration of individuals in IDP camps and SDF prisons remains "the biggest impediment to ensuring the enduring defeat of ISIS."[7]

On September 29, 2021, UN Secretary-General António Guterres announced the launch of a Global Framework for UN Support on Syrian Arab Republic and Iraq Third Country National Returnees to support member states willing to repatriate thousands of what it called foreign terrorist fighters and at least 42,000 foreign, ISIS-linked women and children who remain in overcrowded camps and prisons in Iraq and Syria.[8] The UN Global Framework's status and processes are not clear, but statements made by U.S. and UN officials indicate that the UN is actively working to assist in the repatriation of third-country nationals to their home countries.[9] However, the population in need of repatriation remains at around 2,000.[10]

There are several barriers to the repatriation of the non-Syrians from ISIS prisons, which differ depending on the country.

---

[5] James F. Jeffrey, "ISIS Series: Its Fighters, Prisoners and Future, Part 2: ISIS Prisoners and Families," Wilson Center, December 22, 2020.

[6] Lead Inspector General, 2020b, p. 52.

[7] Lead Inspector General, 2022b, p. 22.

[8] Lead Inspector General, 2021; United Nations, "Launch of the Global Framework for United Nations Support on Syria, Iraq Third Country National Returnees," September 29, 2021.

[9] Michelle Bachelet, "High Commissioner for Human Rights at the High-Level Conference on Human Rights, Civil Society and Counter-Terrorism," Málaga, Spain, May 10, 2022; Richard Mills, "Remarks at a UN Security Council Briefing on Northeast Syria," United States Mission to the United Nations, January 27, 2022.

[10] Savage, 2022; Lead Inspector General, 2020b; Lead Inspector General, 2022b; Lead Inspector General, 2022c.

Iraq

Iraq is one of the few countries playing an active role in repatriating its nationals from SDF detention, and it is doing so with some support from the United States.[11] Iraq has repatriated more than 600 Iraqi ISIS prisoners from SDF custody in northeast Syria.[12] Yet the repatriation effort for ISIS prisoners of Iraqi origin in SDF prisons is only partially complete as an estimated 3,000 ISIS prisoners of Iraqi citizenship remain in SDF facilities.[13]

One barrier to increased repatriation to Iraq is the capacity of the Iraqi justice system itself in comparison with the significant demands on it. Iraq is struggling to fund its legal processes and clear the docket for the many more ISIS prisoners inside Iraq. As of January 2020, Iraq had processed more than 20,000 terrorism cases against ISIS-affiliated suspects.[14] Furthermore, the Iraqi government has requested $1 to $2 million per prosecution for third-country nationals from foreign governments. Iraqi prisoners who are repatriated face a long process. Judicial adjudication backlogs are significant.[15]

At the same time, while fairness of trials are not a topic of study of this paper, UN officials criticize Iraq for the "conduct of the trials and the extraction of confessions under torture" in prosecuting ISIS prisoners and for the

---

[11] Haroro J. Ingram, Julie Coleman, Austin C. Doctor, and Devorah Margolin, "The Repatriation and Reintegration Dilemma: How States Manage the Return of Foreign Terrorist Fighters and Their Families," *Journal for Deradicalization*, No. 31, 2022; Timothy Betts, "Remarks by Timothy Betts (Coordinator for Counterterrorism, U.S. Department of State and U.S Special Envoy to the Global Coalition to Defeat ISIS)," presented at the conference on **Resolving the Detainee Dilemma II: What Next for the Men, Women & Children of Islamic State**, Middle East Institute and International Centre for the Study of Radicalisation, Washington, D.C., July 13, 2022; Dana Stroul, "Remarks by Dana Stroul (Deputy Assistant Secretary of Defense for the Middle East, US Department of Defense)," presented at the conference on **Resolving the Detainee Dilemma II: What Next for the Men, Women & Children of Islamic State**, Middle East Institute and International Centre for the Study of Radicalisation, Washington, D.C., July 13, 2022.

[12] Betts, 2022.

[13] Savage, 2022.

[14] Jo Becker, "Iraq's ISIS Trials Don't Deliver Justice—Including for Children," Human Rights Watch, January 31, 2020.

[15] Ingram et al., 2022.

use of Anti-Terrorism Law Number 13 convictions to carry out mass executions.[16] Trials in Iraq have been reported to last no more than 15 minutes, and the ISIS suspects have been reported to be convicted based on confessions obtained via coercion or torture and without due process protections.[17]

Third-Country National Prisoners

Other countries, including France, the United Kingdom, Australia, Indonesia, Sweden, Canada, Switzerland, Denmark, the Philippines, Serbia, and Albania, have been slow or resistant to extradition. This reluctance stems largely from concerns that home country justice systems are not robust enough to try and sentence ISIS fighters (for example, because evidence needed from Iraq or Syria may be difficult to obtain), concerns that repatriated individuals if not sentenced for life may become responsible for future attacks, concerns over a potential domestic political backlash, concerns over the radicalizing influence of ISIS prisoners in domestic prisons, and concerns about the country's ability to safely monitor those who are extradited or repatriated and released. As an alternative to repatriation, many of these countries have revoked the citizenship of former fighters and their family members in an attempt to relinquish the country from the responsibility of repatriation altogether.

There have recently been a few shifts in the European stance. For example, in 2021, Dutch courts began requiring the government to repatriate citizens who have been charged with terrorism-related offenses to ensure that charges against those offenders are not dropped. This policy appears to have increased the number of Dutch women and children who have been repatriated from camps in Iraq and Syria; however, it is unclear how this may impact those in prisons.[18] Kosovo has repatriated at least 242 individuals and tries all adults it repatriates. Approximately 70 percent of the 124 men

---

[16] United Nations Office of the High Commissioner for Human Rights, "Iraq: Wave of Mass Executions Must Stop, Trials Are Unfair—UN Experts," United Nations, November 20, 2020.

[17] Vera Mironova, *The Challenge of Foreign Fighters: Repatriating and Prosecuting ISIS Detainees*, Middle East Institute, January 2021.

[18] Ingram et al., 2022.

repatriated to Kosovo have been prosecuted, with an average sentence of about 3.5 years. Moreover, Kosovo has established a rehabilitation and reintegration program in its prisons to serve imprisoned former ISIS members.[19] Germany has also convicted ISIS fighters on charges of genocide related to violence and enslavement of the Yazidi population.[20]

Ongoing Instability and Lack of a Political Settlement in Syria

While fighting in Syria's civil war has now subsided, there has been no internationally recognized political settlement to end the fighting formally. The security environment remains weak. Multiple circumstances may make AANES and SDF unable to provide security for the prisons sustainably or make the United States or D-ISIS Coalition partners reluctant to invest in upgraded prisons or prison security capacity:

- **Interference in northeast Syria:** Russia, Iran, and the Assad regime are playing spoilers, while Turkey threatens to invade the northeast.
- **ISIS threats:** ISIS is resurgent throughout Syria, including in the Kurdish northeast, and still presents ongoing security threats, keeping AANES and SDF personnel and infrastructure resources under strain.
- **Inconsistent U.S. commitments:** There is limited U.S. and D-ISIS Coalition presence, and uncertain commitment from the United States to remain over time with different administrations holding different views on the need for U.S. presence. The legal underpinnings for the U.S. and D-ISIS Coalition presence in northeast Syria are tenuous, potentially creating hesitation about investments in prison infrastructure.

---

[19] Ingram et al., 2022.

[20] Bojan Pancevski, "First Yazidi Genocide Trial Ends in Conviction of German ISIS Member," *Wall Street Journal*, October 25, 2021; Amal Clooney, Sonka Mehner, and Natalie von Wistinghausen, "German Court Hands Down Second Genocide Conviction Against ISIS Member Following Enslavement and Abuse of Yazidi Woman in Syria," press release, Doughty Street Chambers, July 28, 2022.

- **Concern over the prisons' future potential use:** There is also concern for how a purpose-built prison might be used if Assad were to take control of northeast Syria.
- **Reliance on a nonstate actor to carry out functions typically performed by states:** There is also a delicate diplomatic balancing act when supporting AANES and SDF as a nonstate actor. Ensuring security in the prisons requires close U.S. coordination with AANES and SDF, as well as caution to ensure that U.S. support does not exacerbate tensions with Turkey, a North Atlantic Treaty Organization ally (e.g., by limiting the types of weapons shared with SDF, avoiding actions that bestow legitimacy on SDF as a nonstate actor, and by avoiding the appearance of seeming to build a state within a state in northern Syria).

Justice Capabilities That Are Unable to Meet Due Process Needs

A robust system to try accused ISIS fighters is lacking. Many capabilities need to be strengthened, including evidence collection processes, capacity to conduct trials for Syrian nationals, juvenile justice procedures for youth, and justice procedures for foreign nationals. In addition, issues related to legitimacy of trials held by AANES need to be resolved.[21] Several key questions in particular need to be addressed: How does international law apply when nonstate actors (AANES and SDF) are required to perform the justice procedures typically undertaken by a recognized sovereign government? What government entity (or entities) has jurisdiction to conduct these varying types of adjudications? Is an internationally recognized and agreed-on tribunal for non-Syrians feasible, and if so, what legal principles should be drawn on?

---

[21] Tanya Mehra and Matthew Wentworth, "New Kid on the Block: Prosecution of ISIS Fighters by the Autonomous Administration of North and East Syria," International Centre for Counter-Terrorism, March 16, 2021.

Capacity of AANES and SDF

One basic barrier to bringing ISIS prisoners to trial is the limited court capacity in northeast Syria. SDF has tried a few hundred low-level Syrian ISIS fighters through the local judicial system, but it lacks the capacity to investigate and try the thousands of other Syrians currently being imprisoned. In October 2020, SDF released 631 prisoners and reduced the terms of 253 prisoners in half as part of a general amnesty for Syrian prisoners who are not linked to violent terrorist acts, honor killings, espionage, or drug trafficking—i.e., prisoners without "blood on their hands."[22] It is unclear how these individuals were identified in terms of eligibility for this relief.

Evidence Collection

While the crimes of ISIS as a group are evident, the evidence needed for individuals' trials has often not been collected and remains difficult to collect. There is a limited window in which to collect such evidence as physical evidence can degrade, be lost, or become tainted (thereby losing its probative value or being deemed inadmissible) due to a lack of proper chain of custody. This is also true of documentary evidence such as identity documents, demographic and medical records, and other government, public, and private records. Additionally, witness testimony in these cases may be critical, but witnesses themselves may become difficult or impossible to locate or may not remember certain relevant facts as time from the pertinent events increases. Also, key classified materials (such as battlefield reports, images, or communication records) from the United States or other D-ISIS Coalition members may be lacking or not accessible because of disclosure prohibitions.

The creation of the UN Investigative Team to Promote Accountability for Crimes Committed by Da'esh/ISIL (UNITAD) in 2018 has sought to improve evidence collection procedures.[23] UNITAD focuses on investigating the war crimes, human rights violations, and genocide committed by ISIS in Iraq and has investigated the use of chemical and biological weap-

---

[22] Lead Inspector General, 2020a, p. 16.

[23] UNITAD, "Our Mandate," webpage, undated.

ons, crimes against minority groups, mass violence, genocide, and crimes against children inside Iraq.[24] However, UNITAD is not a prosecutorial body and does not support AANES and SDF but instead serves to support Iraqi investigations and prosecutions of ISIS members and affiliated individuals regarding their involvement in ISIS human rights violations.[25]

Efforts to collect evidence have also been bolstered by the UN's creation in 2016 of the International, Impartial and Independent Mechanism (IIIM), which supports the investigation and prosecution of individuals complicit in "the most serious crimes under International Law committed in the Syrian Arab Republic since March 2011."[26] The IIIM is responsible for investigating any serious violations of international law in Syria since the outbreak of the Syrian Civil War, regardless of the actor responsible (meaning that the Syrian government, ISIS, and other actors are subject to its investigations). While the IIIM investigates crimes, it has no prosecutorial power and instead supports the prosecution of those responsible for human rights violations in Syria in what it views to be "competent jurisdictions."[27] However, its ability to support AANES and SDF is limited due to concerns over human rights and the UN's inability to recognize AANES as the legitimate governing authority for northeast Syria.

Lack of an Agreed-On Entity to Conduct Justice Procedures for Both Syrians and Foreign Nationals

Any justice procedures for ISIS prisoners would need to be viewed as legitimate by Middle East states, populations of the Middle East, and other stakeholders globally. This legitimacy will depend on which governing author-

---

[24] UNITAD, *Eighth Report of the Special Adviser and Head of the United Nations Investigative Team to Promote Accountability for Crimes Committed by Da'esh/Islamic State in Iraq and the Levant*, United Nations Security Council, May 26, 2022. UNITAD was formed at the request of Iraq to investigate war crimes, human rights violations, and genocide committed by ISIS in Iraq. Syria has not made a similar appeal to the UN. For more, see UNITAD, undated.

[25] UNITAD, undated.

[26] IIIM, "The IIIM," webpage, United Nations, undated-a.

[27] IIIM, "Support to Jurisdictions," webpage, United Nations, undated-b.

ity is recognized as having jurisdiction over both the individuals currently being detained, as well as over the criminal actions they are accused of having committed. In other words, the court or tribunal that adjudicates these cases must have the power to exercise legitimate legal authority over the individuals, as well as the legitimate legal authority to make determinations over the criminal issues in question. Agreeing on (and recognizing) a legitimate authority and a jurisdictional authority concomitant with it will likely be the key challenge for the international community. While there are several options for designating a convenor of trials in northeast Syria—the government of Syria, the UN, and AANES and SDF—they all face limitations:

- If trials were to be held by the Assad government, the results might not be respected or trusted by some states of the world due to the documented failures in the Syrian judicial system.[28]
- The UN is unlikely to sponsor a tribunal for ISIS fighters because it would lack permission from the government of Syria and could be blocked by Russia through the UN Security Council (UNSC). An international UN tribunal would need UN approval (getting around UNSC veto) and Syrian government agreement.[29]
- While the de facto governing authority, prison authority, and convenor of trials in northeast Syria is AANES, AANES is not an internationally or nationally recognized sovereign entity, and SDF is therefore not a state military organization. Previous SDF trials were not recognized as legitimate by the government of Syria or other international entities.[30] Thus, adjudications and decisions by AANES and SDF may, as a practical matter, be null and void in most countries. Assisting AANES

---

[28] See U.S. Department of State, Bureau of Democracy, Human Rights, and Labor, *2020 Country Reports on Human Rights Practices: Syria*, March 30, 2021.

[29] The International Court of Justice has ruled that the UNSC only, and not the UN General Assembly, can establish international tribunals. The UN Charter did not provide the UN General Assembly any judicial authority. See Derek Jinks, "Does the U.N. General Assembly Have the Authority to Establish an International Criminal Tribunal for Syria?" Just Security, May 22, 2014.

[30] Hanna, 2021.

and SDF in conducting justice procedures could mean further legitimizing their administration of the territory, which Turkey views as a threat and would likely oppose. Such assistance may also be viewed as fostering adjudicative processes and decisions that will not ultimately be valid and, therefore, may waste resources.

Lack of a System for Juvenile Justice for ISIS-Affiliated Youth

Finally, there is no detention or adjudicative system to deal with juvenile justice.[31] There is furthermore a lack of consensus surrounding which youth may have committed murder or other crimes as part of ISIS. Should youth be considered victims? Child soldiers? Criminals? Many youth may be in the prisons simply because they are teenage sons of ISIS parents; they may have committed no crimes themselves. Others may have been forced as children to commit crimes. Given the lack of understanding surrounding youth crime, many questions would need to be answered about how a juvenile justice system could be established and implemented.

---

[31] To be compliant with international legal standards for the treatment of juveniles, any judicial system developed would need to adhere to current UN guidelines. See United Nations, 1985.

CHAPTER 4

Courses of Action and Policy Directions

It is likely that at least some of the ISIS prisoners will remain in SDF-controlled facilities for many years, and accordingly, solutions may need to be long term. Reaching a comprehensive solution will depend on answers to open, fundamental questions about the ISIS prisons. We raise five questions that must be addressed to make acceptable outcomes feasible.

- **How can a standard justice process be created for the ISIS prisoners?** Answering this question requires consideration of standard processes for trying and punishing prisoners, venues for and staffing of such tribunals, rules of evidence, and cost estimates for different potential solutions.
- **If ISIS prisoners remain in northeast Syria, how can adequate security and minimum prison standards be sustained?** This would require upgrading facilities and procedures to meet these goals, along with long-term commitments for resources and technical assistance from the D-ISIS Coalition.
- **If ISIS prisoners were to be moved out of northeast Syria and not repatriated to their home nations, where could the prisoners be held and who would guard and manage them?** Important decisions include whether isolated, internationally run facilities could be created; whether repatriated fighters should be put into special facilities in their home countries; and whether multinational support for such facilities should be provided.
- **What options are available for youth over the long term?** Even with education and training, young prisoners will lack the necessary docu-

ments (such as proof of identity, travel authorizations, proof of education, and medical information) to enable them to live normal lives in society and the formal economy. Stigma is likely to follow many of them for their entire lives. An important question is how to balance support for these young people with support for the many other young people whose lives ISIS has damaged but who were involved even peripherally with an extremist group.

- **What should happen to Syrian ISIS prisoners?** As long as the civil war is unresolved, sending them back to Assad-controlled territory may expose them to horrific conditions of torture in Syrian prisons, or could enable Assad to weaponize them for future conflict. But releasing them into the northeast could result in strengthening ISIS activities in that area.

Although these questions may lack answers, there are steps that can be taken in the short and medium term to address many of the troubling issues raised by the current situation. In this section, we first discuss potential short-term actions—those that can be done within one year—and then medium-term policy directions—those that could be carried out within the following two to five years. These actions were described by participants in the policy summit, sometimes supplemented by the literature review and other analyses conducted for this project. Many of these actions should be undertaken by D-ISIS coalition members; it is unlikely that the UN would be able to do so given divisions within the UNSC, the Assad regime's prevailing international recognition as the government in Syria, and the nature of these tasks. The United States is currently in the lead, but European and even other regional countries could take a higher profile. Other actions will be the responsibility of AANES or SDF and governments of countries from which presumed ISIS fighters have come. Finally, AANES and the D-ISIS Coalition should collaborate with international NGOs when appropriate to implement these recommendations.

Short-Term Actions (One Year)

Recognize the Long-Term Nature of This Prison Population and Conduct Prison Census

Organizations with any responsibility or involvement in the ISIS prisons must first acknowledge that at least some, potentially many, of these presumed-ISIS prisoners will remain in these facilities for the medium to long term. Some former ISIS fighters will likely need to remain imprisoned for the rest of their lives to preserve regional and global security. This acknowledgment is foundational to recognizing the need for ISIS prisons to reflect the Mandela Rules regarding security and humanitarian standards.[1] Conducting a census of prisoners would provide SDF and the D-ISIS Coalition a better understanding of the prison population and its needs. A consistent barrier discussed to improving conditions and instituting justice processes in a way that would ensure appropriate punishment was the imprecise nature of the total number of presumed ISIS-fighters imprisoned by SDF. Because conflicting and potentially outdated numbers exist in the public sphere, a census would also support establishing processes and pathways for solutions for prisoners.

Conduct Security Assessments to Understand Threats, Set Priorities

Previous efforts and current security and living conditions within the prisons must be assessed to determine the prioritization of resources, operations, activities, and investments related to the prisons. Identifying security gaps and requirements for improving internal and external prison conditions can establish the basis for understanding the full scope of the situation facing SDF and the D-ISIS Coalition. In the interim, current efforts to provide security assistance and minimum prison standard support should continue. This includes basic life support services, security force stipends, prison construction support, guard and security force training, and sustainment.[2]

---

[1] See generally, United Nations Office of the High Commissioner for Human Rights, 2022.

[2] Office of the Secretary of Defense, 2022.

Assess and Encourage Repatriation or Return Efforts

Efforts to encourage repatriation of foreign prisoners should continue. Separate inducements might be needed for European nationals and for other non-Iraqi foreign nationals, as well as the development of justice processes, described below. Iraq has indicated willingness to repatriate its nationals and has done so on a modest scale. Through accelerated diplomacy, the D-ISIS Coalition should work with the government of Iraq to determine what barriers are preventing the further repatriation of the remaining fighters and help Iraq to address them, even if additional investments in Iraqi justice capacity are required.

An important step would be to work with the Europeans to repatriate their citizens. Much of this will involve a policy discussion within European countries and within the European Union, but active, behind-the-scenes diplomacy by the United States should continue to be exercised to maintain pressure or explore alternatives. Discussion at our workshop reflected views that European police and justice authorities could handle the prisoners, so (at least in some cases) action may depend on political authorities making the decision to repatriate.

For the Syrian fighters, facilitating their return to their home region or to a more permanent and secure location is more complicated, as the country remains unstable. ISIS fighters came from across all of Syria, not simply the northeast. With the country in civil conflict, returning any released fighters to regime-controlled areas could lead to their weaponization against the D-ISIS Coalition or in acts of violence to carry out other policy goals of the Assad government. The SDF previously worked with tribes in northeastern Syria to release hundreds of Syrian ISIS-affiliated prisoners who repudiated ISIS and were determined not to have committed crimes.[3] Unfortunately, information is sparse regarding their post-release status. In the short term, an internationally led assessment should build on these efforts to identify locations where released prisoners could return, establish a formalized system to review releases, and determine the current status of the previously released prisoners, including whether they are pursuing a nonviolent course

---

[3] "Syria Kurds Free More Than 600 ISIL Fighters as Part of Amnesty," 2020; Jeff Seldin, "In Syria, Captured Islamic State Fighters, Followers Going Home," *VOA*, January 23, 2020.

of life or whether they have rejoined ISIS in any way. Understanding what that process entails and formalizing it could be an effective exit strategy, especially if those previously released did not rejoin the group.

Develop Justice Processes

Currently, foreign national prisoners might face trial in their home countries, while Syrian prisoners could face a potentially ill-defined process. An assessment of existing justice processes can provide guidance on the type of justice process needed to determine the guilt or innocence of presumed-ISIS prisoners and could lead to judgments and convictions that respect international norms and values.

The assessment should also determine where such a court should be located, whether there should be multiple courts, and what the status of evidence collection is related to ISIS-perpetrated crimes. For example, establishing a Syria-based justice system could influence currently recalcitrant countries to repatriate their citizens. Any assessment of justice processes is unlikely to be led by the UN; support from the Assad regime is unlikely and the chance of a Russian veto in the UNSC is high.

Related to the establishment of a justice process, the IIIM or NGOs will likely need to be partnered with or hired to gather and process evidence that is ready for trial.[4] Additionally, the United States and necessary allies and partners should, in concert with law enforcement and military authorities, commence the review of intelligence and begin declassifying that information to support trials.

Move Youth from Prisons to Facilities Designed to Support Their Unique Needs

The presumed ISIS-affiliated youth, both those immediately imprisoned following their departure from Baghouz and those transferred from IDP camps as they reach their teenage years, need special consideration apart

---

[4] Regarding support for judicial proceedings by NGOs, see generally, Human Rights Watch, "How National Nongovernmental Organizations Can Work with the Court," in *The International Criminal Court: How Nongovernmental Organizations Can Contribute to the Prosecution of War Criminals*, September 2004.

from the adults. In the short term, youth need to be transferred from the prisons and placed into facilities specially designed to house youth and support their educational and healthcare needs. Whether the center in Qamishli is the best location to house the youth will need to be assessed, and it should not be simply another holding facility for youth without addressing unique needs and improving the living conditions in which they are held accordingly.

Moreover, processes should be developed to determine which youth are radicalized or may have committed crimes as Cubs of the Caliphate. In concert with age-appropriate education, rehabilitation assessments and services must be established and available to address physical and psychological trauma and radicalized views. There are lessons or good practices that can be drawn from other situations involving conscription of child soldiers.[5]

Medium-Term Policy Directions (Two to Five Years)

Construct Purpose-Built Prisons That Meet International Standards While Continuing to Professionalize Security Forces

While much can be done in one year, new construction takes longer. The Western members of the D-ISIS Coalition have experience building prisons that can comply with the Mandela Rules.[6] They should consider doing so in northeast Syria, at a minimum to improve security. While the United States (or another single country with a prison construction industry) could be responsible for supervision of the actual construction, another option is for counter-ISIS coalition members to pool funds to pay for construction. This would likely require a separate funding mechanism other than humanitarian and recovery assistance or further adjustments made to the CTEF authorization.

---

[5] Some of these lessons can be found in International Centre for Counter-Terrorism and International Organization for Migration, *Roundtables on Prosecution, Rehabilitation and Reintegration*, The Hague and Baghdad, 2022.

[6] For a list of prison projects in the United States, see Construction Market Data, "Prison Information," webpage, Construction Connect, 2018.

Once built, the prisons might be managed or comanaged by the United States and D-ISIS Coalition members in coordination with the northeast Syria governing authorities, which would relieve pressure on SDF and the PrISF. However, such a management structure might be politically difficult for D-ISIS Coalition members and could represent a recurring expense that they are reluctant to take on. In addition, the northeast Syria authorities might not welcome such comanagement, as it might involve a lower level of control for them. AANES and SDF will still need to take the lead on staffing the prisons. And if they were to continue with full management of the prisons, D-ISIS Coalition members should at minimum provide technical support. Options for managing and supporting the prisons could also include collaboration with other Middle Eastern states.

The biggest obstacle is that any construction would need to be done over the objections of the Syrian government. However, countries operating against ISIS are already taking actions in Syria over the objections of the Syrian government, and prison construction might be justified under the D-ISIS campaign. It is unlikely that any new prison construction would receive approval from the UN, so this effort would need to be carried out under D-ISIS Coalition auspices. A second obstacle is the risk of the Assad government inheriting the prisons if it took over northeast Syria. Torture is routine in Syrian government prisons.[7] The coalition would likely want to avoid the risk of giving the Assad government new facilities in which to torture. In response to these concerns, D-ISIS Coalition authorities would need to be ready to dismantle the prisons should they risk falling into Syrian government control.

Implement Repatriation and Justice Processes That Reflect International Standards

As noted above, repatriation efforts, which have been ongoing since the end of the territorial caliphate in 2019, should be an important part of the short-term actions. But repatriation is unlikely to be completed and possibly not even arranged by the end of 2023, and developing justice procedures may

---

[7] Anne Barnard, "Inside Syria's Secret Torture Prisons: How Bashar al-Assad Crushed Dissent," *New York Times*, May 11, 2019.

likewise take time. Accordingly, these efforts should be an important part of medium-term policy directions.

International technical assistance may be useful to improve the standards of Iraqi justice processes, and that could take time. Funding for this could be included either in civilian aid or in security assistance. Even so, a case can be made that, even under current conditions, Iraq should be encouraged to repatriate its citizens held in the northeast Syria prisons. Not unlike ISIS fighters captured, imprisoned, and tried in Iraq, those Iraqi fighters captured in Syria should remain subject to Iraqi judicial systems, especially as judicial processes remain nascent in northeastern Syria. The more difficult problem would be to establish justice processes for ISIS prisoners from countries other than Iraq and Syria. Ideally, countries should repatriate their citizens and put them through their own national justice systems or deradicalization programs. Such actions are possible, as demonstrated by Central Asian countries.[8]

One option short of repatriation could be the development of an international process with internationally run prisons for those found guilty of ISIS-related crimes. These prisons could be separate and in isolated locations, following the Guantanamo model, recognizing the myriad challenges of extraterritorial court and prison locations, and improving on these challenges based on historic lessons learned. In the short term, countries would need to define such a process and collect evidence. In the medium term, the challenge would largely be one of implementation. Elements of this include process, funding, and staffing. There are previous models on which countries can rely, including the Nuremberg trials for Nazi authorities, the war crimes trials for World War II-era Japanese authorities, the International Criminal Tribunal for the former Yugoslavia, the International Criminal Tribunal for Rwanda, and the International Residual Mechanism for Criminal Tribunals.[9] However, ISIS trials are likely to involve a far larger number of people than these tribunals did, and so funding may be the biggest obstacle because of the sheer numbers of people who will need to be tried. In this

---

[8] William B. Farrell, Rustam Burnashev, Rustam Azizi, and Bakhtiyar Babadjanov, *Processes of Reintegrating Central Asian Returnees from Syria and Iraq*, Special Report No. 498, United States Institute of Peace, July 2021.

[9] United Nations, "International Residual Mechanism for Criminal Tribunals," webpage, undated.

case, countries that refuse to repatriate their citizens, such as most European countries, could be responsible for the bulk of financing. Beyond funding, a variety of issues must be defined, including different courses of action for ISIS leadership versus regular members, due process rules, defense representation, and identification of prosecutors and judges. Creating and implementing such a tribunal is predicated on the idea that leaving the ISIS prisoners in place would be far more dangerous and costly.

Determine Exit Pathways for Youth

As noted above, the short-term task would be to move youth to separate, more humane facilities and instituting age-appropriate services, such as improved living conditions, physical and mental health access, and education in line with the rights of the child.[10] In the medium term, youths' education will need to continue (or even start in some cases), and they will need to build skills that will allow them to support themselves when released. Part of their education should include deradicalization for those who need it and socialization into normal social practices. As with all other issues, this will take funding, personnel, and care to get it right.

Youth will need documentation attesting to their education and identity. Eventually they will need to be placed, since they should not be detained indefinitely. This placement could occur when they become adults and age out of a youth facility, or it could occur when they are still minors if countries or families are willing to take them.

The main obstacle is likely to be the possibility that no country is willing to take them. Communities in Syria may also not be welcoming, leaving these youth without families and with a pariah status in Syria. Figuring out how and where to place them and integrate them into future lives is an area for further work.[11]

---

[10] United Nations, 1989.

[11] One ongoing challenge in determining resource allocation to the youth in ISIS prisons is that youth throughout the region have been badly affected by war and also would benefit from assistance. A discussion of numerous policy considerations, including those facing youth in ISIS prisons, can be found in Alex Fischer, Haid Haid, and James Khalil, *Youth Disrupted: Impact of Conflict and Violent Extremism on Adolescents in Northeast Syria*, Cross-Border Evidence, Policy, Trends, September 2022.

CHAPTER 5

Conclusion

The nations of the Middle East and the broader international community have faced the quandary of ISIS prisoners in northeast Syrian prisons since the fall of Baghouz and the end of the territorial caliphate in March 2019. The fact that there has been only modest resolution of the problem—in the form of some repatriation of ISIS fighters to Iraq and elsewhere—suggests that there are politically difficult roadblocks or that solutions may be costly in the short term. Accordingly, the default approach has been to maintain the prisons—to leave the ISIS fighters in Northeast Syria under the control of the financially weak, nonstate AANES in conditions that meet neither security requirements nor minimum prison standards. However, the short-term benefit of doing this is likely to be outweighed by the long-term cost if the ISIS prisoners successfully break free and help the group reconstitute.

Our policy summit discussions suggested that there are potential solutions to the prisoner dilemma and that a plan for working towards such solutions can be created, with short-term actions and medium-term policy directions. These range from leaving ISIS fighters in place in prisons in northeast Syria—with upgrades to and hardening of the prisons, as well as better training and equipping of guards—to repatriating foreign prisoners to their home countries while establishing judicial processes that adhere to international norms and standards. These discussions also suggested that without further internationalization of the problem and possibly increased funding to the AANES and SDF, there is little prospect that the situation can be ameliorated, although there has been only muted interest from around the world for increasing the level of international involvement and funding.

As of late 2022, the conditions for solving the problem of ISIS prisoners in northeast Syria was not favorable. A new Turkish military operation in northern Syria and Iraq, dubbed Operation Claw-Sword, in November

41

2022 provided a strong reminder.[1] In the face of Turkish airstrikes and a potential ground operation, SDF said in late November that it had halted operations against ISIS and threatened to stop guarding IDP camps, such as al-Hol, although it was not clear whether the threat extended to the prisons.[2] However, there are concrete steps that can be taken in the course of one to five years. A grand coalition defeated a great evil with the final assault on Baghouz. Follow-up by that same coalition can ensure the group does not reconstitute and return.

---

[1] Kristina Jovanovski, "Turkey Says Ground Incursion into Syria Imminent Despite U.S., Russian Concerns," The Media Line, November 23, 2022.

[2] On the halt in operations against ISIS, see Robert Tollast, ""Syrian Kurds Say Anti-ISIS Operations Stopped Amid Turkish Attack," *The National*, November 27, 2022. On the threat to cease guard operations, see Poonam Taneja and Jewan Abdi, "Islamic State: Kurdish Forces Threaten to Stop Guarding Camps," BBC, November 25, 2022.

Abbreviations

AANES	Autonomous Administration of North and East Syria
COVID-19	coronavirus disease 2019
CTEF	Counter-ISIS Train and Equip Fund
D-ISIS	Defeat-ISIS
DoD	U.S. Department of Defense
IDP	internally displaced person
IIIM	International, Impartial and Independent Mechanism
InSF	Internal Security Forces
ISA	International Security Affairs
ISIS	Islamic State of Iraq and Syria
NGOs	nongovernmental organizations
PKK	Kurdistan Workers Party
PrISF	Provincial Internal Security Forces
SDF	Syrian Democratic Forces
UN	United Nations
UNITAD	United Nations Investigative Team to Promote Accountability for Crimes Committed by Da'esh/ISIL
UNSC	United Nations Security Council

References

Abadi, Cameron, "Why Is Turkey Fighting Syria's Kurds?" *Foreign Policy*, October 17, 2019.

Arraf, Jane, and Sangar Khaleel, "Teenage Inmates Found Among the 500 Dead in Syria Prison Attack," *New York Times*, January 31, 2022.

Bachelet, Michelle, "High Commissioner for Human Rights at the High-Level Conference on Human Rights, Civil Society and Counter-Terrorism," Málaga, Spain, May 10, 2022.

Barnard, Anne, "Inside Syria's Secret Torture Prisons: How Bashar al-Assad Crushed Dissent," *New York Times*, May 11, 2019.

Becker, Jo, "Iraq's ISIS Trials Don't Deliver Justice—Including for Children," Human Rights Watch, January 31, 2020.

Betts, Timothy, "Remarks by Timothy Betts (Coordinator for Counterterrorism, U.S. Department of State and U.S Special Envoy to the Global Coalition to Defeat ISIS)," presented at the conference on Resolving the Detainee Dilemma II: What Next for the Men, Women & Children of Islamic State, Middle East Institute and International Centre for the Study of Radicalisation, Washington, D.C., July 13, 2022.

Blinken, Antony J., "Secretary Antony J. Blinken Opening Remarks at D-ISIS Meeting Opening Session," ministerial meeting of the Global Coalition to Defeat ISIS, Rome, Italy, June 28, 2021.

"Calls to Evacuate 700 Boys from Syria's Guweiran Prison Due to Intense Fighting," press release, Save the Children, January 24, 2022.

Clifford, Bennett, and Caleb Weiss, "'Breaking the Walls' Goes Global: The Evolving Threat of Jihadi Prison Assaults and Riots," *Combating Terrorism Center Sentinel*, Vol. 13, No. 2, February 2020.

Clooney, Amal, Sonka Mehner, and Natalie von Wistinghausen, "German Court Hands Down Second Genocide Conviction Against ISIS Member Following Enslavement and Abuse of Yazidi Woman in Syria," press release, Doughty Street Chambers, July 28, 2022.

Combined Joint Task Force—Operation Inherent Resolve, "Coalition: Iran-Backed Militia Attacks a Dangerous Distraction from Mission," January 5, 2022.

Construction Market Data, "Prison Information," webpage, Construction Connect, 2018. As of August 23, 2022:
https://www.cmdgroup.com/building-types/prisons/all/

Dettmer, Jamie, "Steeped in Martyrdom, Cubs of the Caliphate Groomed as Jihadist Legacy," *VOA*, July 6, 2017.

Farrell, William B., Rustam Burnashev, Rustam Azizi, and Bakhtiyar Babadjanov, *Processes of Reintegrating Central Asian Returnees from Syria and Iraq*, Special Report No. 498, United States Institute of Peace, July 2021.

Fischer, Alex, Haid Haid, and James Khalil, *Youth Disrupted: Impact of Conflict and Violent Extremism on Adolescents in Northeast Syria,* Cross-Border Conflict Evidence, Policy, Trends, September 28, 2022.

Fishman, Brian, *Fourth Generation Governance—Sheikh Tamimi Defends the Islamic State of Iraq*, Combating Terrorism Center, West Point, March 23, 2007.

Fore, Henrietta, "Children Caught Up in al-Hasakah Prison Violence Must Be Evacuated to Safety," press release, United Nations Children's Fund, January 25, 2022.

Gilmour, Andrew, "The Nelson Mandela Rules: Protecting the Rights of Persons Deprived of Liberty," *United Nations Chronicle*, undated.

Gordon, Michael R., *Degrade and Destroy: The Inside Story of the War Against the Islamic State, from Barack Obama to Donald Trump*, Farrar, Straus, and Giroux, 2022.

Hanna, Andrew, "Islamists Imprisoned Across the Middle East," Wilson Center, June 24, 2021.

al-Hashimi, Hisham, Telegraph Interactive Team, and Ruth Sherlock, "Revealed: The Islamic State 'Cabinet,' from Finance Minister to Suicide Bomb Deployer," *The Telegraph*, July 9, 2014.

Hassan, Mohammed, and Samer al-Ahmed, "Iran's Growing Presence in Syria's al-Hasakah Poses a Direct Threat to U.S. Forces," Middle East Institute, March 24, 2022.

Human Rights Watch, "How National Nongovernmental Organizations Can Work with the Court," in *The International Criminal Court: How Nongovernmental Organizations Can Contribute to the Prosecution of War Criminals*, September 2004.

Humud, Carla E., "Syria and U.S. Policy," Congressional Research Service, IF 11930, updated April 19, 2022.

IIIM—*See* International, Impartial, and Independent Mechanism.

Ingram, Haroro J., Julie Coleman, Austin C. Doctor, and Devorah Margolin, "The Repatriation and Reintegration Dilemma: How States Manage the Return of Foreign Terrorist Fighters and Their Families," *Journal for Deradicalization*, No. 31, 2022.

International Centre for Counter-Terrorism and International Organization for Migration, *Roundtables on Prosecution, Rehabilitation and Reintegration*, The Hague and Baghdad, 2022.

International, Impartial, and Independent Mechanism, "The IIIM," webpage, United Nations, undated-a. As of August 31, 2022:
https://iiim.un.org/

International, Impartial, and Independent Mechanism, "Support to Jurisdictions," webpage, United Nations, undated-b. As of August 31, 2022:
https://iiim.un.org/what-we-do/support-to-jurisdictions/

Jeffrey, James, "Assessing the Impact of Turkey's Offensive in Northeast Syria," Hearing before the Committee on Foreign Relations, United States Senate, Senate Hearing 116-109, October 22, 2019.

Jeffrey, James F., "ISIS Series: Its Fighters, Prisoners and Future, Part 2: ISIS Prisoners and Families," Wilson Center, December 22, 2020.

Jinks, Derek, "Does the U.N. General Assembly Have the Authority to Establish an International Criminal Tribunal for Syria?" Just Security, May 22, 2014.

Johnston, Patrick B., Jacob N. Shapiro, Howard J. Shatz, Benjamin Bahney, Danielle F. Jung, Patrick K. Ryan, and Jonathan Wallace, *Foundations of the Islamic State: Management, Money, and Terror in Iraq, 2005–2010*, RAND Corporation, RR-1192-DARPA, 2016. As of August 18, 2022:
https://www.rand.org/pubs/research_reports/RR1192.html

Jovanovski, Kristina, "Turkey Says Ground Incursion into Syria Imminent Despite U.S., Russian Concerns," The Media Line, November 23, 2022.

al-Khateb, Khaled, "Is Russia Extorting SDF in Northeast Syria?" *Al-Monitor*, February 26, 2021.

Lead Inspector General, *Operation Inherent Resolve: Lead Inspector General Report to the United States Congress, October 1, 2019–December 31, 2019*, U.S. Department of Defense, February 4, 2020a.

Lead Inspector General, *Operation Inherent Resolve: Lead Inspector General Report to the United States Congress, July 1, 2020–September 30, 2020*, U.S. Department of Defense, November 3, 2020b.

Lead Inspector General, *Operation Inherent Resolve: Lead Inspector General Report to the United States Congress, July 1, 2021–September 30, 2021*, U.S. Department of Defense, November 3, 2021.

Lead Inspector General, *Operation Inherent Resolve: Lead Inspector General Report to the United States Congress, October 1, 2021–December 31, 2021*, U.S. Department of Defense, February 8, 2022a.

Lead Inspector General, *Operation Inherent Resolve: Lead Inspector General Report to the United States Congress, January 1, 2022–March 31, 2022*, U.S. Department of Defense, May 3, 2022b.

Lead Inspector General, *Operation Inherent Resolve: Lead Inspector General Report to the United States Congress, April 1, 2022–June 30, 2022*, U.S. Department of Defense, July 29, 2022c.

Lewis, Jessica, "Al Qaeda in Iraq's 'Breaking the Walls' Campaign Achieves Its Objectives at Abu Ghraib," 2013 Iraq Update #30, Institute for the Study of War, July 28, 2013.

Lister, Charles, "Who's Who of the Islamic State Senior Leadership," in *Profiling the Islamic State*, Brookings Institution, December 1, 2014.

Loft, Philip, *Syria and Its Civil War: A Future Under Assad?* Commons Library Research Briefing Number 9378, House of Commons Library, United Kingdom, November 26, 2021.

Loveluck, Louisa, "The World Forgot This Syrian Prison. The Islamic State Did Not." *Washington Post*, February 5, 2022.

Loveluck, Louisa, and Sarah Cahlan, "Prison Break: ISIS Fighters Launched a Brazen Attack to Free Their Comrades," *Washington Post*, February 3, 2022.

Malsin, Jared, and Benoit Faucon, "Islamic State Plotted Comeback Long Before Syria Prison Attack," *Wall Street Journal*, January 28, 2022.

Mehra, Tanya, and Matthew Wentworth, "New Kid on the Block: Prosecution of ISIS Fighters by the Autonomous Administration of North and East Syria," International Centre for Counter-Terrorism, March 16, 2021.

Mills, Richard, "Remarks at a UN Security Council Briefing on Northeast Syria," United States Mission to the United Nations, January 27, 2022.

Mironova, Vera, *The Challenge of Foreign Fighters: Repatriating and Prosecuting ISIS Detainees*, Middle East Institute, January 2021.

Murdock, Heather, "Foreign Children of IS Detained in Northeast Syria Face Bleak Future," *VOA*, November 4, 2021.

Ní Aoláin, Fionnuala, "Position of the United Nations Special Rapporteur on the Promotion and Protection of Human Rights and Fundamental Freedoms While Countering Terrorism on the Human Rights of Adolescents/Juveniles Being Detained in North-East Syria," United Nations Human Rights Special Procedures, May 2021.

Oehlerich, Eric, Mick Mulroy, and Liam McHugh, *Jannah or Jahannam: Options for Dealing with ISIS Detainees*, Middle East Institute, October 13, 2020.

Office of the Secretary of Defense, *Department of Defense Budget Fiscal Year (FY) 2023: Justification for FY 2023 Overseas Operations Counter-Islamic State of Iraq and Syria (ISIS) Train and Equip Fund (CTEF)*, U.S. Department of Defense, April 2022.

Pancevski, Bojan, "First Yazidi Genocide Trial Ends in Conviction of German ISIS Member," *Wall Street Journal*, October 25, 2021.

Said, Rodi, "Islamic State 'Caliphate' Defeated, Yet Threat Persists," Reuters, March 23, 2019.

Savage, Charlie, "As ISIS Fighters Fill Prisons in Syria, Their Home Nations Look Away," *New York Times*, July 18, 2018.

Savage, Charlie, "ISIS Fighters' Children Are Growing Up in a Desert Camp. What Will They Become?" *New York Times*, July 19, 2022.

Seldin, Jeff, "In Syria, Captured Islamic State Fighters, Followers Going Home," *VOA*, January 23, 2020.

Shirzada, Noorullah, and Elise Blanchard, "Islamic State Jihadists on the Run After Afghan Prison Raid," AFP, August 4, 2020.

Stroul, Dana, "Remarks by Dana Stroul (Deputy Assistant Secretary of Defense for the Middle East, US Department of Defense)," presented at the conference on Resolving the Detainee Dilemma II: What Next for the Men, Women & Children of Islamic State, Middle East Institute and International Centre for the Study of Radicalisation, Washington, D.C., July 13, 2022.

"Syria: 700 Child Detainees Held in Prison Under Siege," UN News, January 25, 2022.

"Syria Kurds Free More Than 600 ISIL Fighters as Part of Amnesty," *Al Jazeera*, October 15, 2020.

Taneja, Poonam, and Jewan Abdi, "Islamic State: Kurdish Forces Threaten to Stop Guarding Camps," BBC, November 25, 2022.

Tollast, Robert, "Syrian Kurds Say Anti-ISIS Operations Stopped Amid Turkish Attack," *The National*, November 27, 2022.

UNITAD—*See* United Nations Investigative Team to Promote Accountability for Crimes Committed by Da'esh/ISIL.

United Nations, "International Residual Mechanism for Criminal Tribunals," webpage, undated. As of August 24, 2022:
https://www.irmct.org/en

United Nations, *United Nations Standard Minimum Rules for the Administration of Juvenile Justice (The Beijing Rules)*, Adopted by General Assembly Resolution 40/33 of November 29, 1985.

United Nations, *Convention on the Rights of the Child*, Adopted by General Assembly Resolution 44/26 of November 20, 1989.

United Nations, "Launch of the Global Framework for United Nations Support on Syria, Iraq Third Country National Returnees," September 29, 2021.

United Nations General Assembly, *The United Nations Standard Minimum Rules for the Treatment of Prisoners (the Nelson Mandela Rules)*, Adopted by the General Assembly Resolution 70/175 of December 17, 2015.

United Nations Investigative Team to Promote Accountability for Crimes Committed by Da'esh/ISIL, "Our Mandate," webpage, undated. As of August 31, 2022:
https://www.unitad.un.org/content/our-mandate

United Nations Investigative Team to Promote Accountability for Crimes Committed by Da'esh/ISIL, *Eighth Report of the Special Adviser and Head of the United Nations Investigative Team to Promote Accountability for Crimes Committed by Da'esh/Islamic State in Iraq and the Levant,* May 26, 2022.

United Nations Office of the High Commissioner for Human Rights, "Iraq: Wave of Mass Executions Must Stop, Trials Are Unfair—UN Experts," November 20, 2020.

United Nations Office of the High Commissioner for Human Rights, "International Standards on Detention," webpage, undated. As of November 26, 2022:
https://www.ohchr.org/en/detention/international-standards-detention

United Nations Security Council, "ISIL/Da'esh Committed Genocide of Yazidi, War Crimes Against Unarmed Cadets, Military Personnel in Iraq, Investigative Team Head Tells Security Council," press release, May 10, 2021.

U.S. Department of Defense and U.S. Department of State, *Foreign Military Training Report, Fiscal Years 2020 and 2021: Joint Report to Congress, Volume 1,* October 18, 2021.

U.S. Department of Defense Inspector General, *Audit of the DoD's Accountability of the Counter-Islamic State of Iraq and Syria Train and Equip Fund Equipment Designated for Syria*, U.S. Department of Defense, DODIG-2020-061, February 13, 2020.

U.S. Department of State, "Members—The Global Coalition to Defeat ISIS," webpage, undated. As of November 27, 2022:
https://www.state.gov/the-global-coalition-to-defeat-isis-partners/

U.S. Department of State, "Senior State Department Officials on the Situation in Syria," briefing, Office of the Spokesperson, October 10, 2019.

U.S. Department of State, Bureau of Democracy, Human Rights, and Labor, *2020 Country Reports on Human Rights Practices: Syria*, March 30, 2021.

Weiss, Caleb, "Islamic State Claims Prison Break in the DRC," *Long War Journal*, Foundation for Defense of Democracies, October 20, 2020.